Advent A-Z

26 DAYS OF
HAND LETTERING
WITH THE SAINTS

Lorelei Worland
Books Faith Life

Copyright © 2019 Lorelei Worland
www.BooksFaithLife.com

For details and order information, contact the author Lorelei@BooksFaithLife.com

All rights reserved. No part of this book may be reproduced or transmitted in any form or by any means whatsoever without express written permission from the author, except in the case of brief quotations embodied in critical articles and reviews.

About the Author

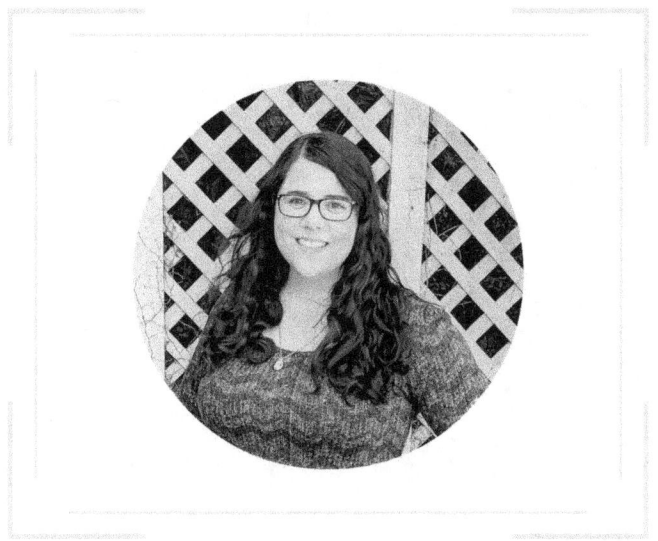

Lorelei has designed and sold beautiful goods through her store, Books Faith Life Shop, since 2017. Her products have appeared in Radiant Magazine and at charitable auctions. She delights in finding new books, old Catholic traditions, and sweet white wines. Lorelei lives with her husband, son, and lazy dachshund on the sunny Mississippi gulf coast.

You can find more about her and her work at booksfaithlife.com

Anatomy of a Letter

1. Baseline

The line where all letters rest. Shown in dark grey.

2. Meanline

The midline where lowercase letters without ascenders terminate. Shown in light grey.

3. Cap line

The line where uppercase letters terminate. Shown in dark grey.

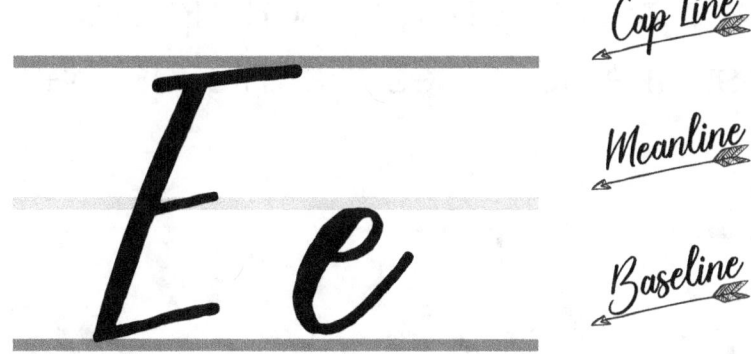

Anatomy of a Letter

4. Ascender

The part of the letter that goes above the midline.

5. Descender

The part of the letter that dips below the baseline.

6. Upstroke

The upward stroke of the letter. By **decreasing** pressure on your soft-tip brush pen, the upstroke becomes the thinnest part of the letter.

7. Downstroke

The downward stroke of the letter. By **increasing** gentle pressure on your soft-tip brush pen, the downstroke becomes the thickest part of the letter.

Ff Gg Mm Qq

Supplies needed:

1. Brush pen

You will need a **soft-tip** brush pen to create the thick & thin lines characteristic of modern hand lettering. This is the only must-have writing implement for this workbook.

My favorite brush pens are the Tombow™ Fudenosuke Soft Tips. They're smooth and flexible enough to finish this workbook with ease.

You can buy individual pens from craft stores for around $3.

2. Scratch paper

While you have lots of space for practice, I like to warm up my letterforms on scratch paper first. A smooth premium printer paper is the most economical choice. Or for the best effect, use a marker or watercolor paper.

Let's Get Started

Think of this book as an Advent calendar. Each day you'll open to the next letter, and a new Saint quote to practice lettering. You can also color in the decorative wreaths and bouquets. The quote pages are single sided, so you can cut them out and display your work.

Be patient with your progress. Remember, the true treasure is the of words of the Saints.

Finally, you can download extra practice pages at www.booksfaithlife.com/practice

Go slowly. Practice often. Most of all, have fun!

> As much as love grows in you, so beauty grows.
> For love itself is the beauty of the soul.
> *St Augustine*

The First Week of Advent

Under Pressure

As we learned in the introduction, the defining look of brush lettering is one of thick downstrokes and slender upstrokes. Random, variable stroke thickness looks unbalanced.

The theory is straightforward. When your pen is moving downward, exert a steady, slightly firm pressure. This brings the thicker portion of your pen nib down to the paper. The result is a wider line.

Whenever your pen moves horizontally (like crossing a t), or moves upward, release the pressure. These low-pressure strokes use just the narrow tip of your pen nib, creating a graceful line.

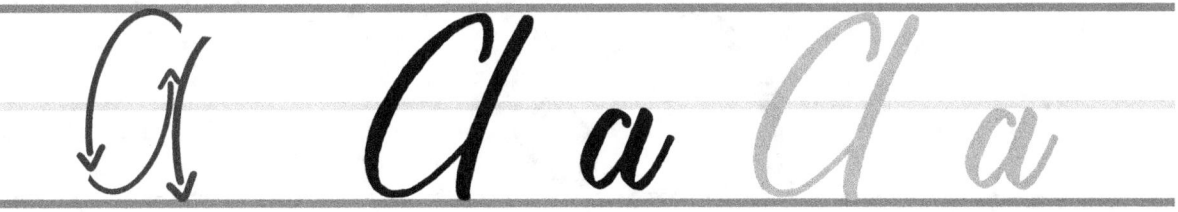

Getting consistent strokes with smooth transitions takes time and effort. There's no substitute for practice.

Begin releasing pressure before the transition. Your pen nib needs time to spring back.

Gently release pressure before the curve to flow into a narrow upstroke. This will smoothly narrow the thick line into a triangle at the bottom of the downstroke,

This week, pay close attention to the direction of your pen's movement when choosing pressure.

Be sure to practice your strokes (up, down, horizontal, diagonal, and circles) on scratch paper. You are training the muscles in your hand, wrist, and arm. With practice, you will create consistent pressure for steady lines and transitions.

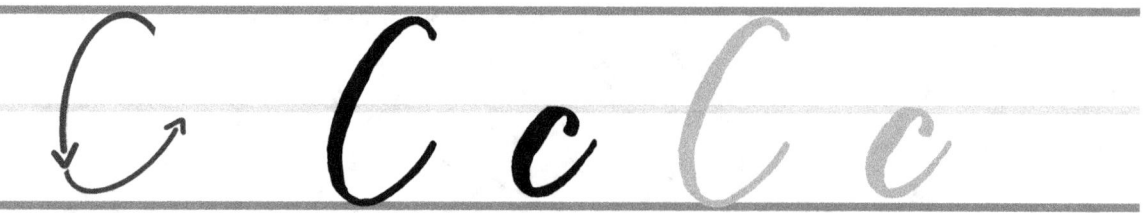

Aa

A A A A A A

A A A A A A

a a a a a a a

a a a a a a a

Augustine

Aa

A A A A A A

A A A A A A

a a a a a a a

a a a a a a a

Augustine

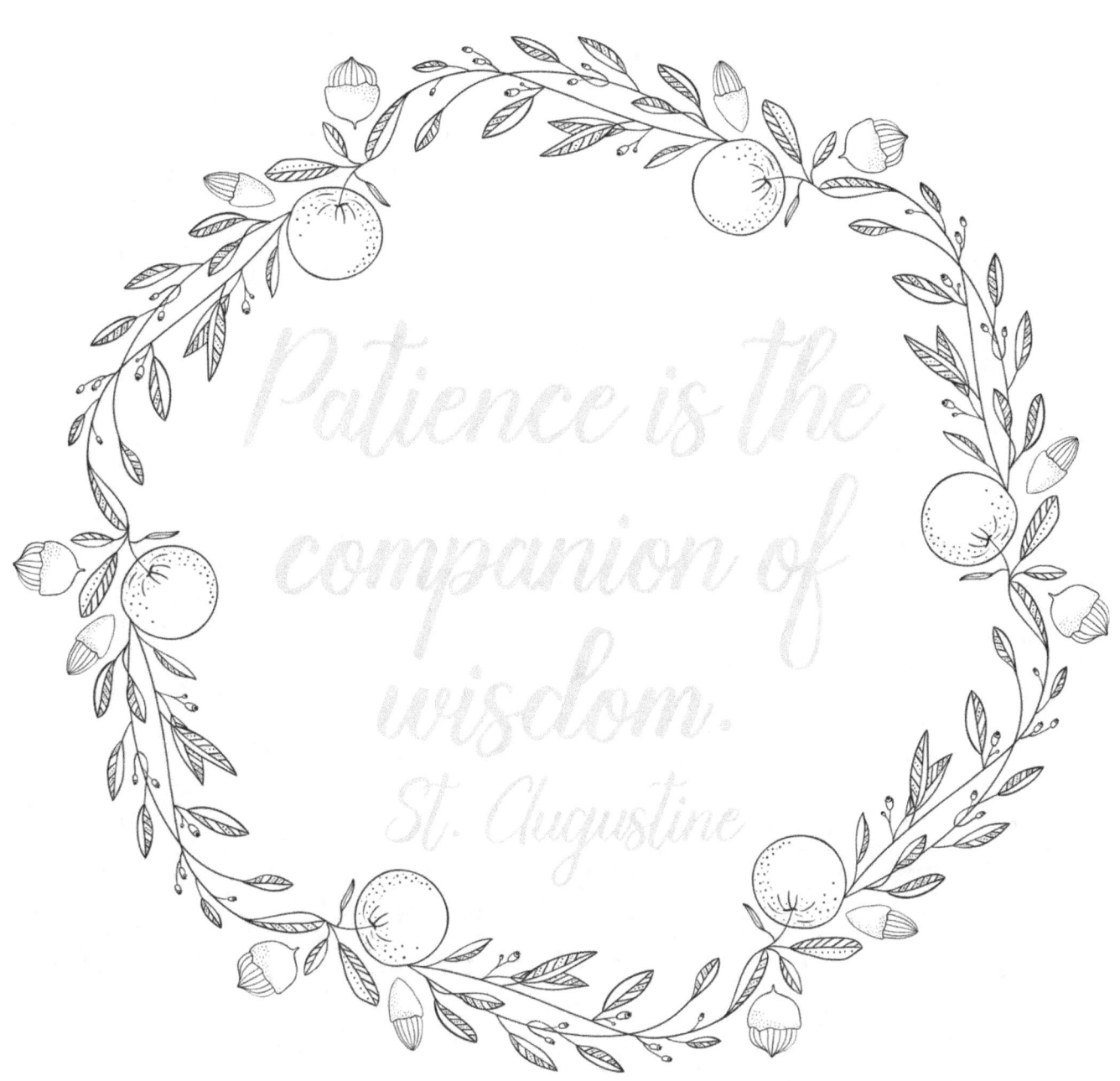

Patience is the companion of wisdom.
St. Augustine

Bb

B B B B B

B B B B B

b b b b b b b

b b b b b b b

Bernard

Bb

B B B B B

B B B B B

b b b b b b b

b b b b b b b

Bernard

Wait upon the Lord.
Be faithful to His
commandments.
He will elevate your
hope, and put you
in possession of
His Kingdom.
St. Bernard of Clairvaux

Cc

C C C C C

C C C C C

c c c c c c c

c c c c c c c

Clare

Cc

C C C C C

C C C C C

c c c c c c c

c c c c c c c

Clare

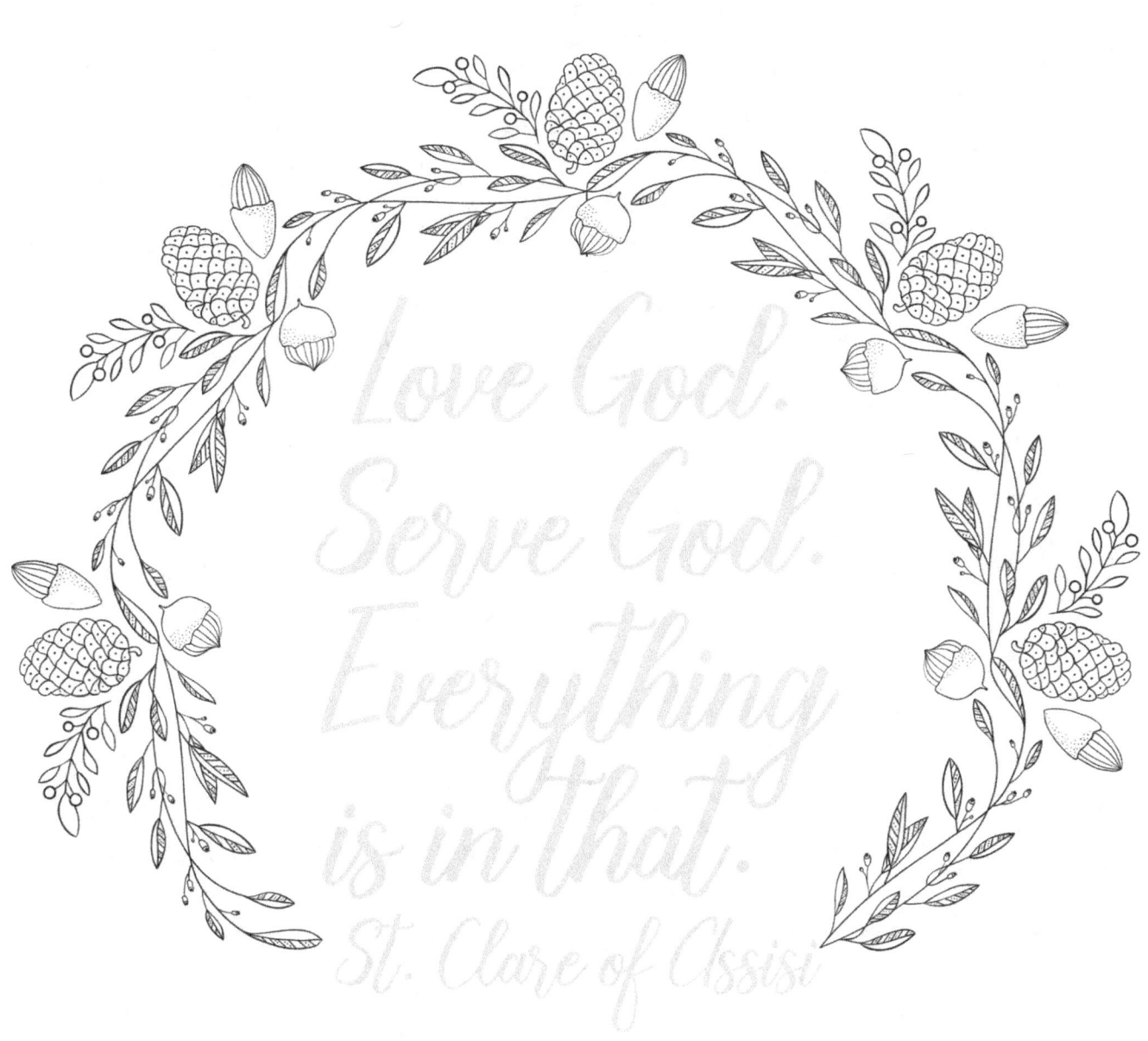

Love God.
Serve God.
Everything
is in that.
St. Clare of Assisi

Dd

D D D D D

D D D D D

d d d d d

d d d d d

Dominic

Dd

D D D D D

D D D D D

d d d d d

d d d d d

Dominic

Arm yourself with prayer rather than a sword. Wear humility rather than fine clothes.
— St. Dominic

Ee

E E E E E

E E E E E

e e e e e

e e e e e

Elizabeth

Ee

E E E E E

E E E E E

e e e e e

e e e e e

Elizabeth

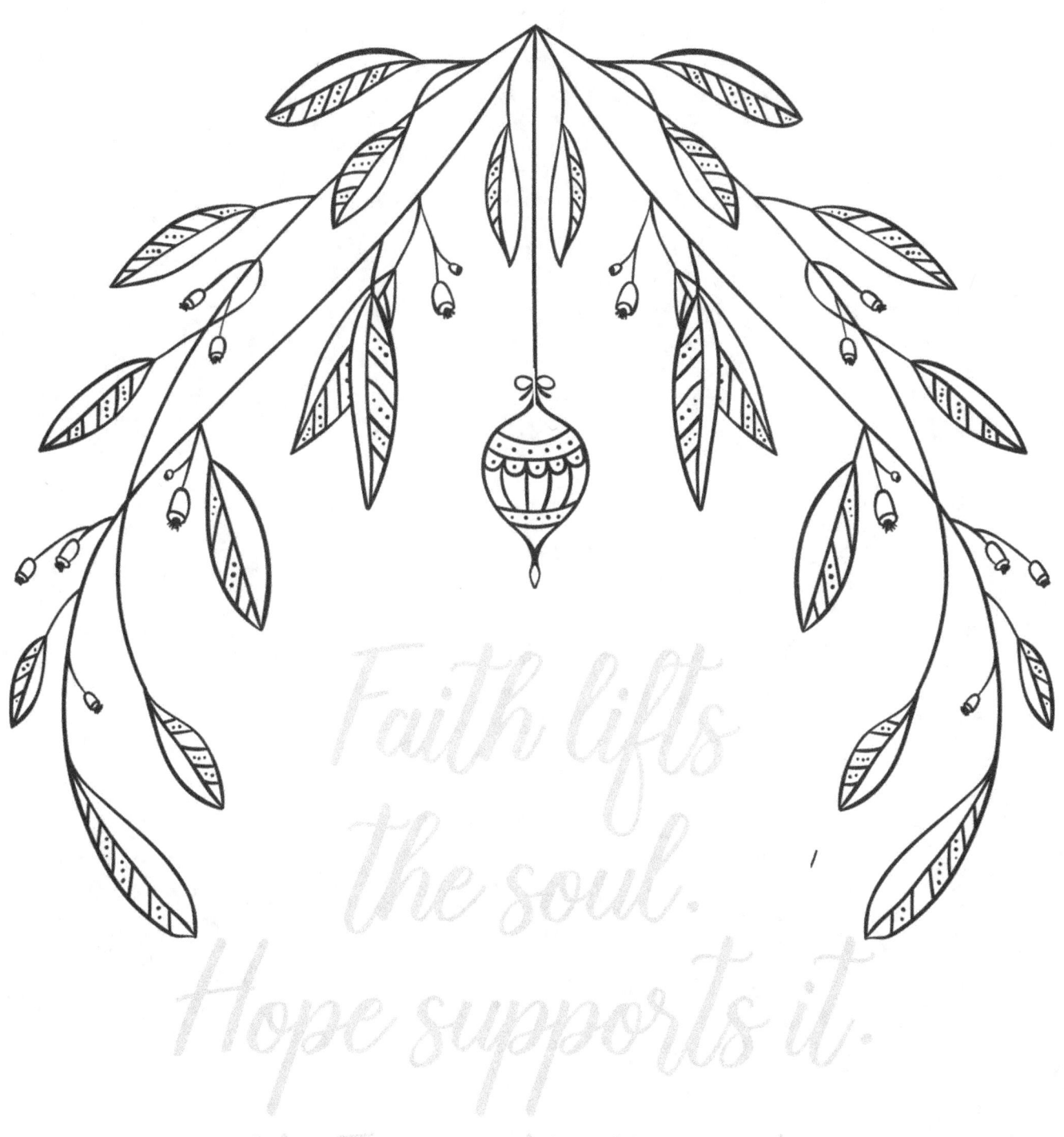

Ff

F F F F F

F F F F F

f f f f f

f f f f f

Francis

Ff

F F F F F

F F F F F

f f f f f

f f f f f

Francis

All the darkness in the world cannot extinguish the light of a single candle.

— St. Francis of Assisi

Gg

G G G G G

G G G G G

g g g g g

g g g g g

Gregory

Gg

G G G G G

G G G G G

g g g g g

g g g g g

Gregory

*Give something,
however small,
to the one in need.
For it is not small
to one who has
nothing.*
— St. Gregory Nazianzen

The Second Week of Advent

Take a Break

When we learned cursive in school, we were told to not take our pencil off the page. Hand lettering is more like painting than writing though. You need to take your brush off the page frequently.

These pauses allow you to adjust pressure, evaluate your progress, and make corrections going forward.

Your pen might leave the page before every downstroke, between each letter, or even more often. Do what feels and looks right to you.

Don't worry about finishing quickly. Your speed will improve with practice. Even experienced letterers take it slow, and letter more slowly than writing in manuscript.

This week, be sure to let your pen leave the page.

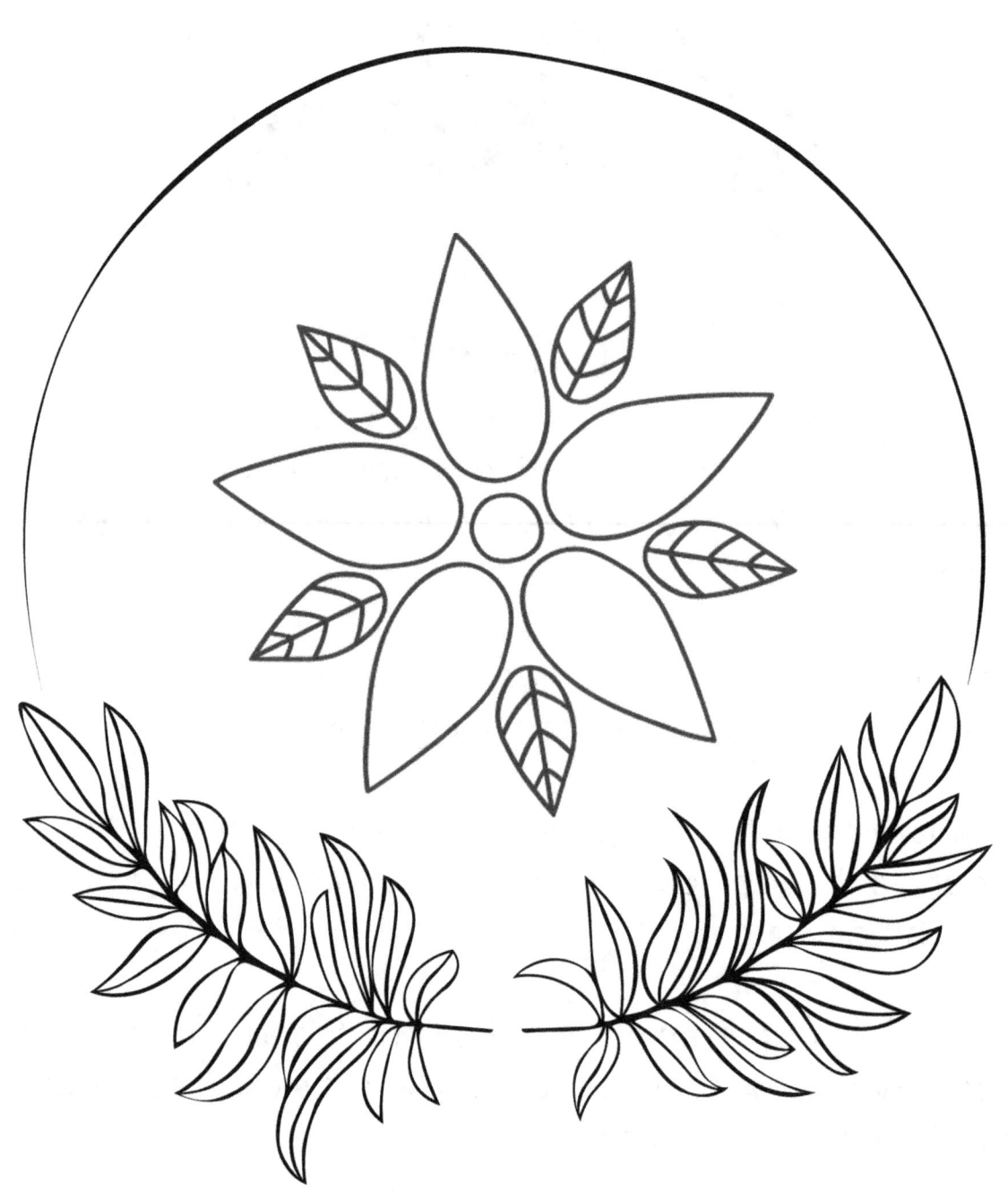

Hh

H H H H H H

H H H H H H

h h h h h h

h h h h h h

Hildegard

Hh

H H H H H

H H H H H

h h h h h

h h h h h

Hildegard

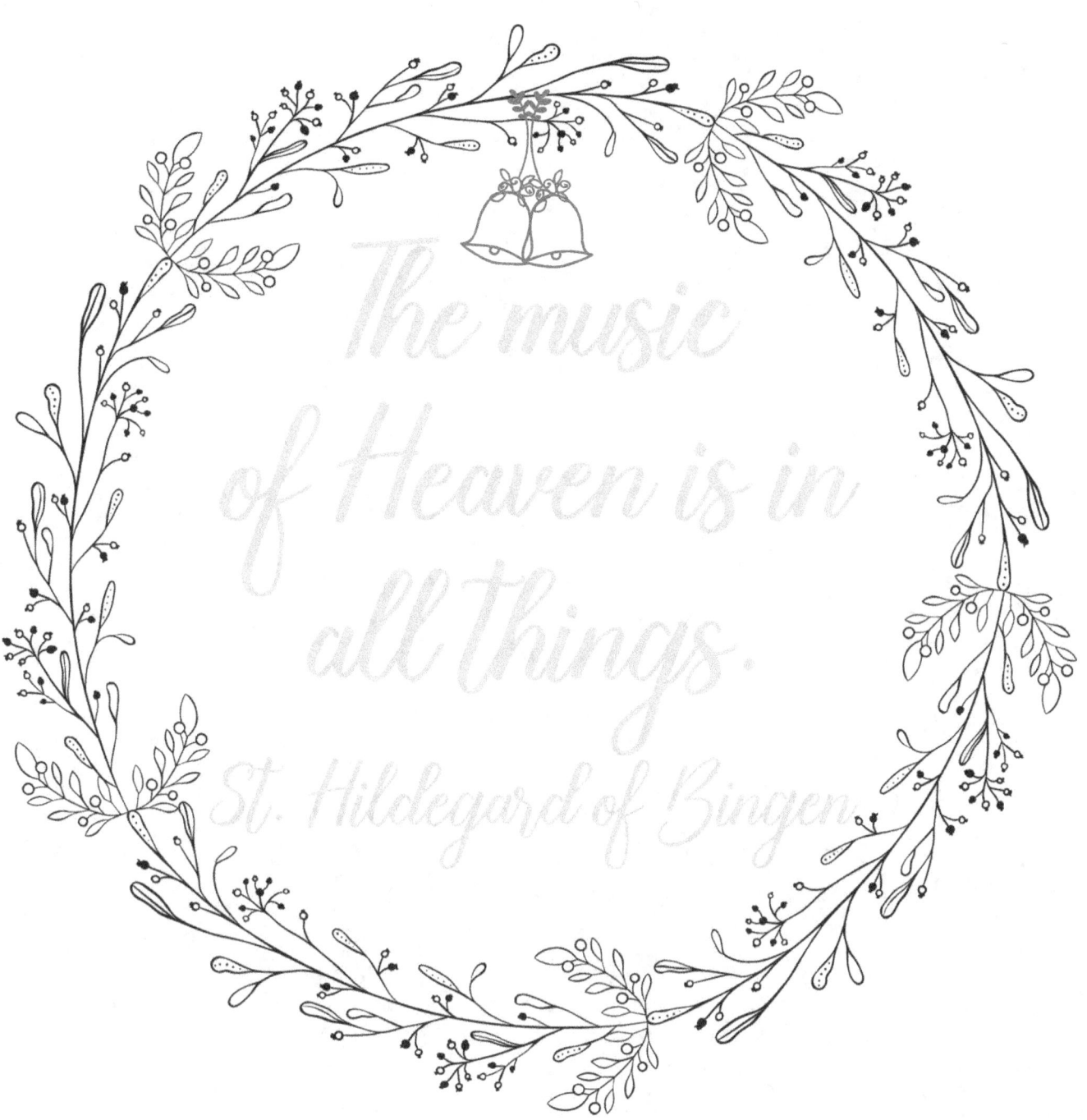

The music of Heaven is in all things.
St. Hildegard of Bingen

Ii

I I I I I

I I I I I

i i i i i

i i i i i

Ignatius

Ii

I I I I I

I I I I I

i i i i i

i i i i i

Ignatius

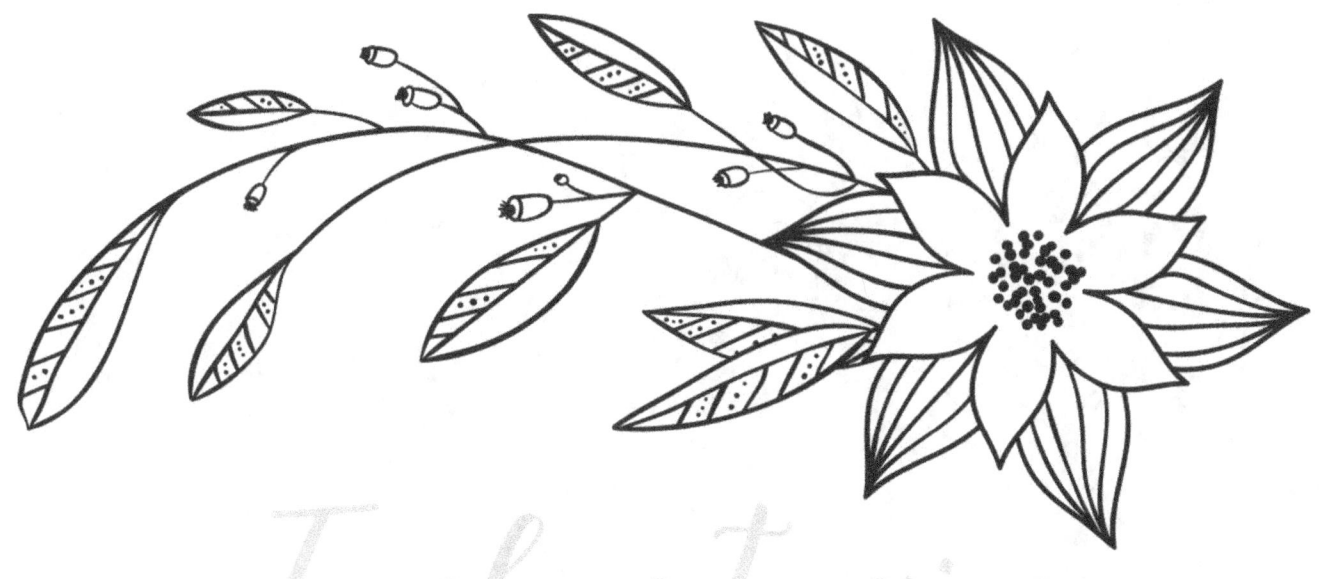

Teach us to give and not count the cost.

St. Ignatius of Loyola

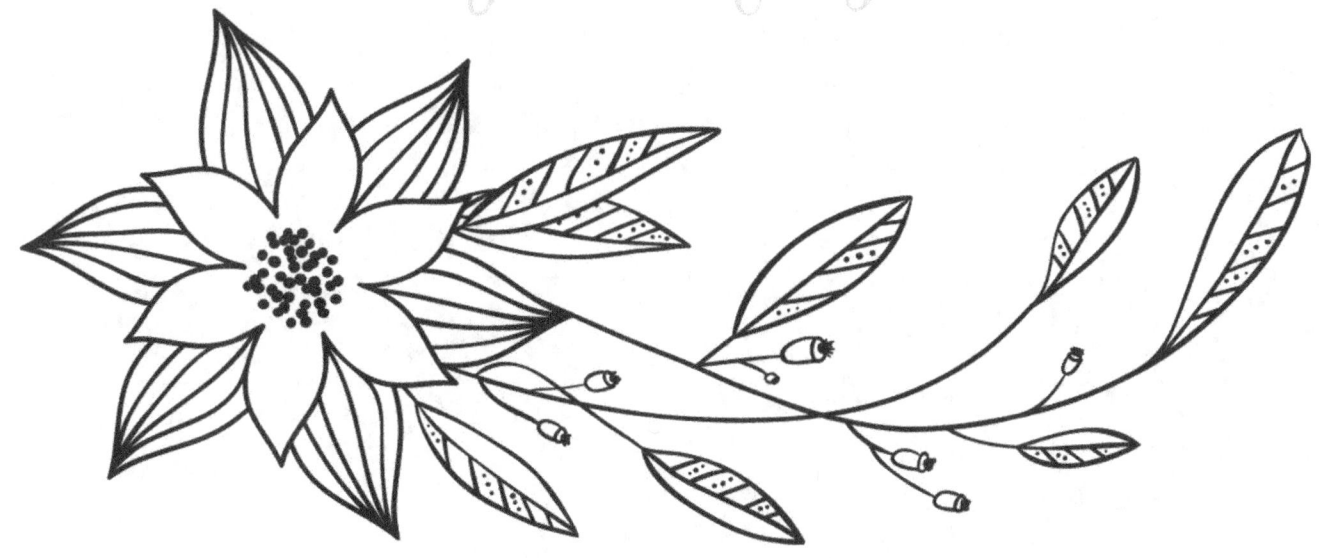

Jj

J J J J J J

J J J J J J

j j j j j j

j j j j j j

Jane

Jj

J J J J J

J J J J J

j j j j j

j j j j j

Jane

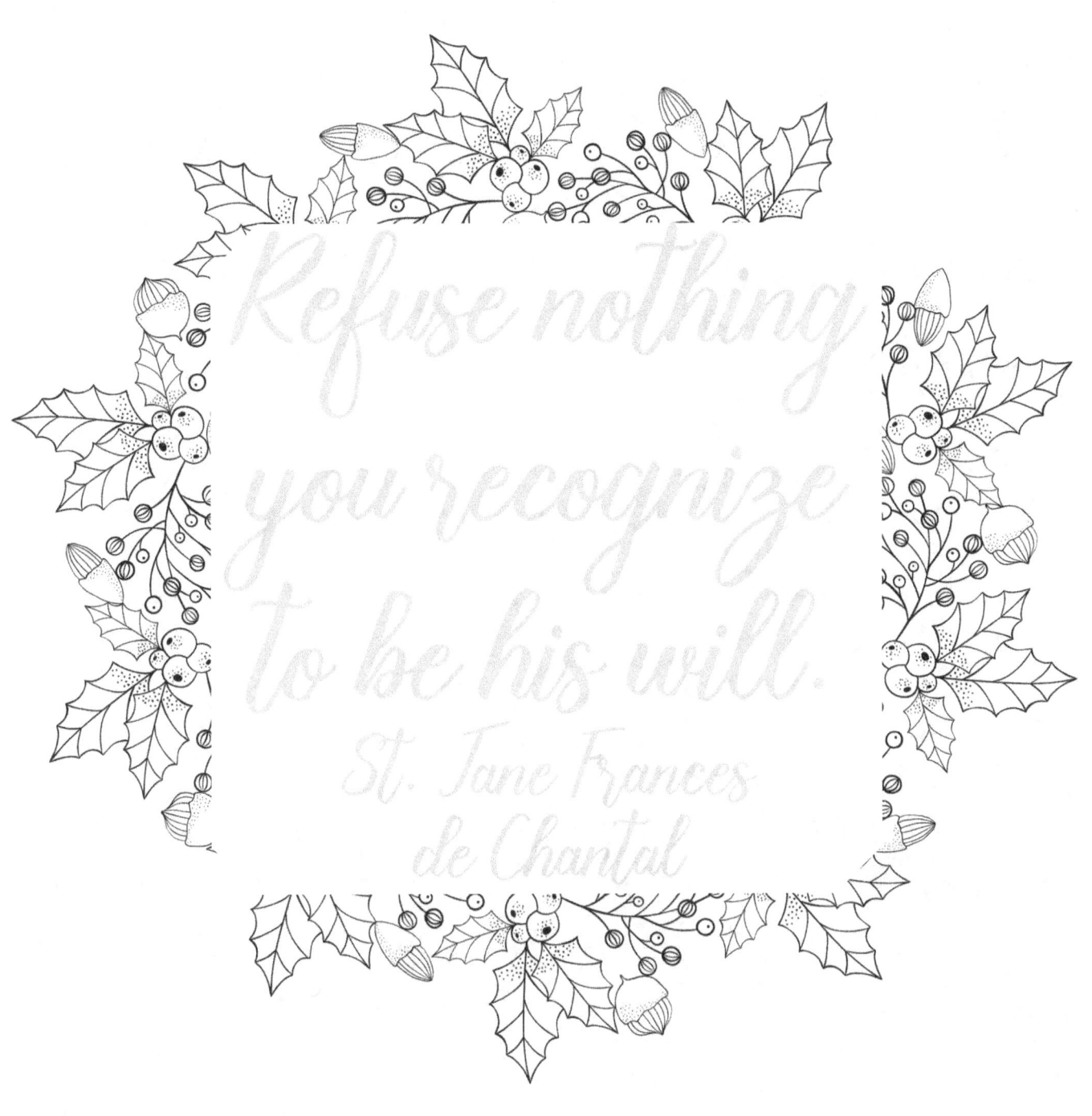

Refuse nothing you recognize to be his will.
St. Jane Frances de Chantal

Kk

K K K K K

K K K K K

k k k k k

k k k k k

Katharine

Kk

K K K K K

K K K K K

k k k k k

k k k k k

Katharine

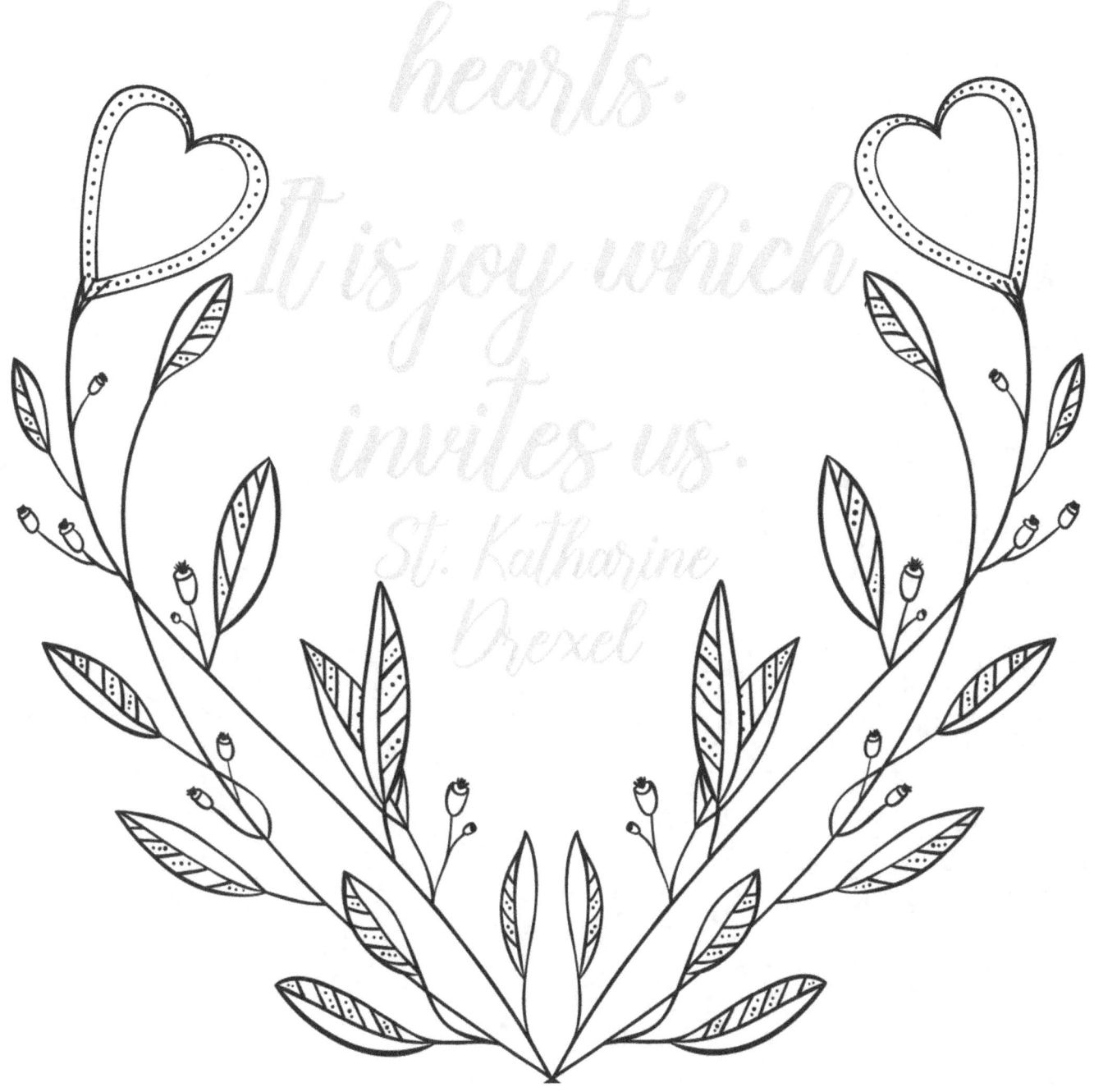

Let us open wide our hearts. It is joy which invites us.
St. Katharine Drexel

Ll

L L L L L

L L L L L

l l l l l

l l l l l

Louis

Ll

L L L L L

L L L L L

l l l l l

l l l l l

Louis

God is a spring of living water which flows unceasingly into the hearts of those who pray.
— St. Louis de Montfort

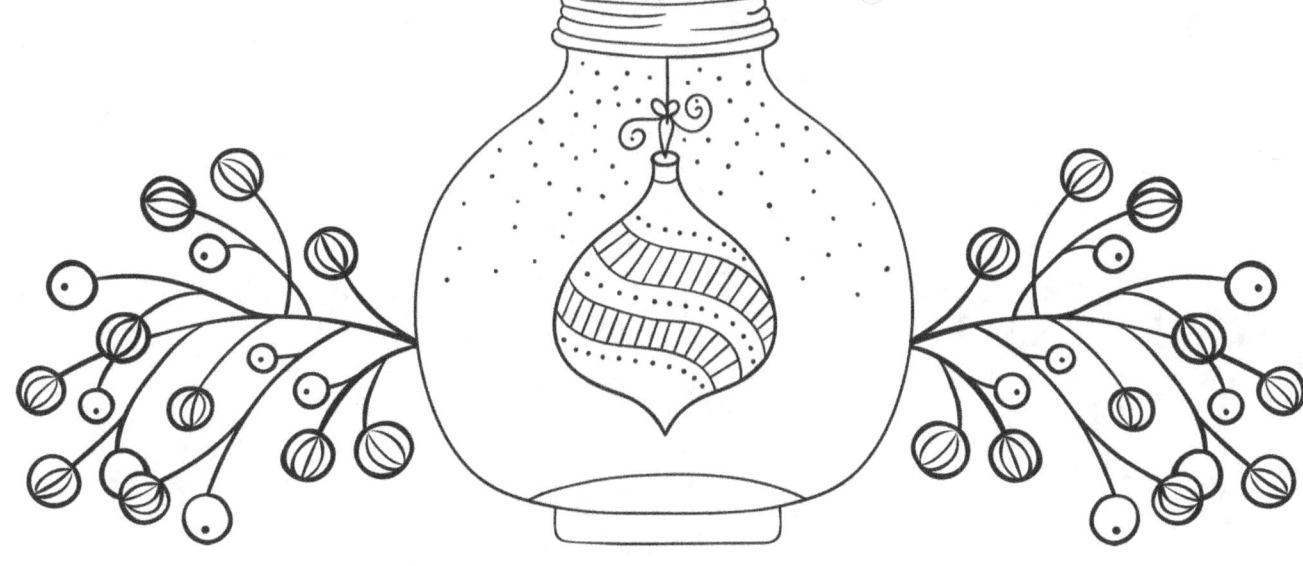

M m

M M M M M M

M M M M M M

m m m m m m

m m m m m m

Mary

M m

M M M M M M

M M M M M M

m m m m m

m m m m m

Mary

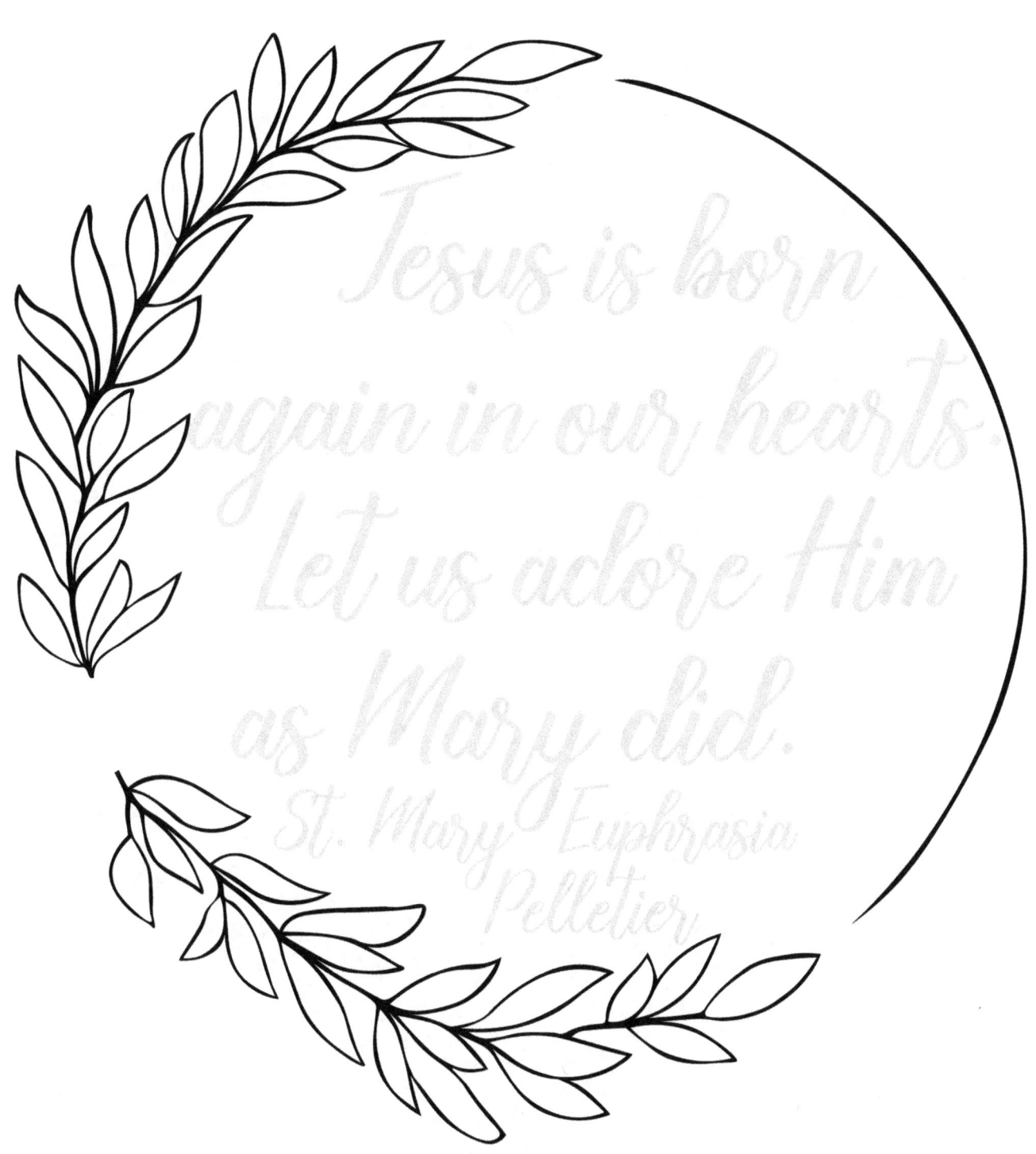

Jesus is born again in our hearts. Let us adore Him as Mary did.
St. Mary Euphrasia Pelletier

Nn

N N N N N

N N N N N

n n n n n

n n n n n

Nicholas

Nn

N N N N N

N N N N N

n n n n n

n n n n n

Nicholas

The giver of every
good and perfect gift
has called upon us to
mimic God's giving
by grace,
through faith.
St. Nicholas of Myra

The Third Week of Advent

Be Kind to Your Pens

Don't damage your pen nibs. A frayed or misshapen nib will mess up all your hard work.

Don't push too hard. Yes, the base of the pen must be in contact with the paper to form thick downstrokes. But to preserve the quality of the nib, you want to use the least force neccesary. Experiment on scratch paper to find the correct pressure.

Always use smooth paper. A smooth premium printer paper is the most economical choice. Or for the best effect, use marker paper or watercolor paper.

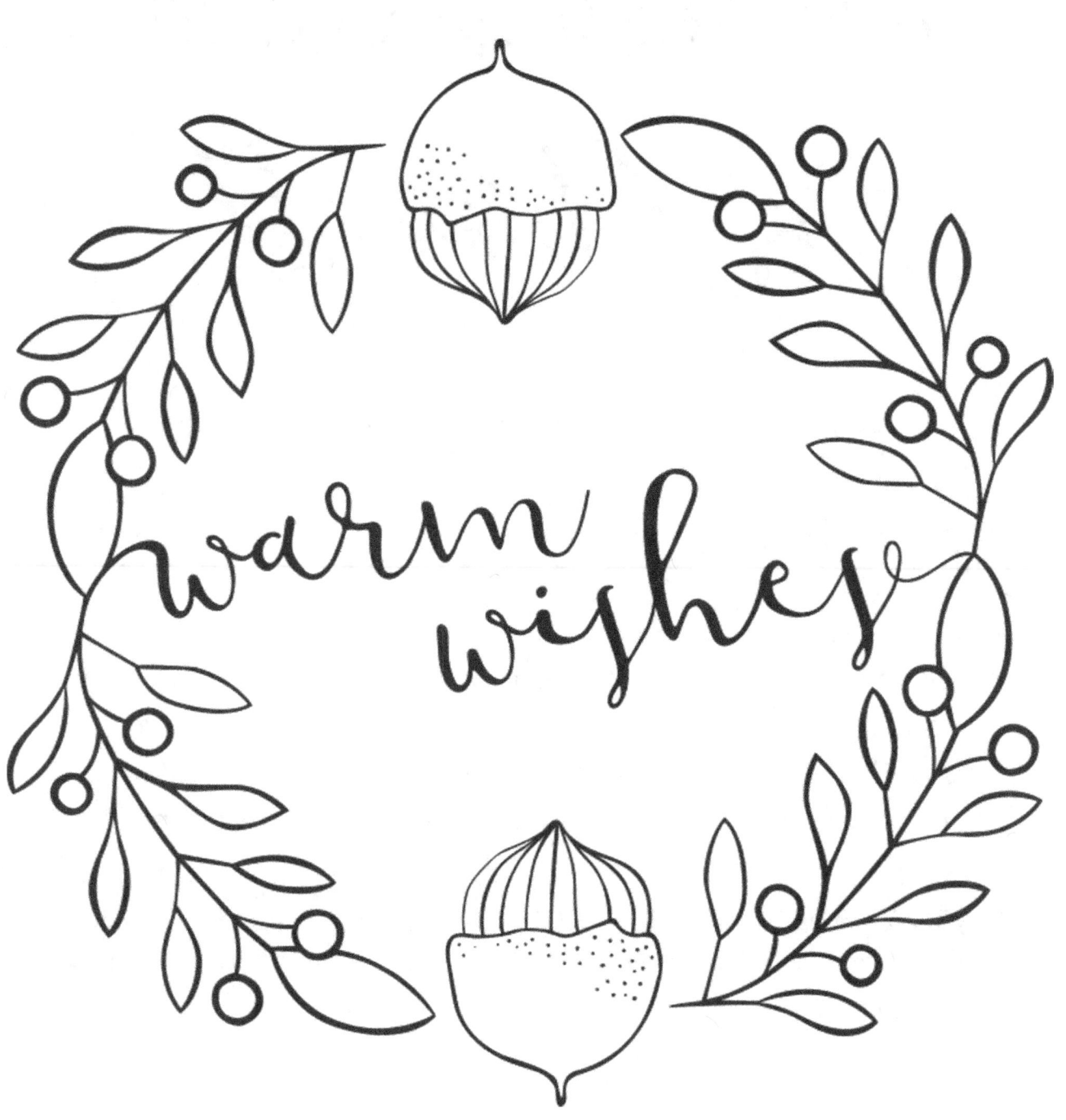

Oo

O O O O O

O O O O O

o o o o o

o o o o o

Our Lady

Oo

O O O O O

O O O O O

o o o o o

o o o o o

Our Lady

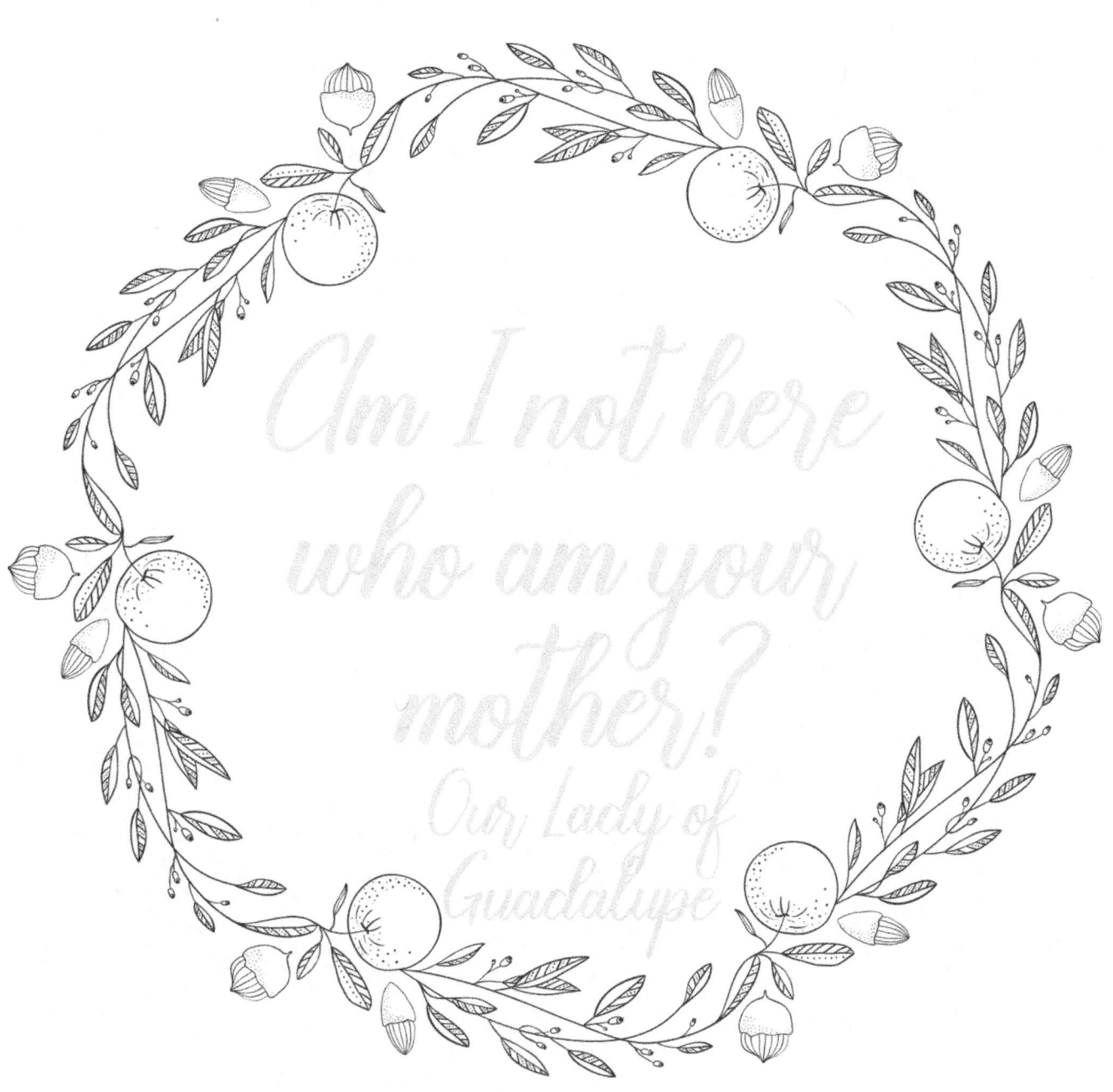

Pp

p p p p p

p p p p p

p p p p p

p p p p p

Padre Pio

Pp

p p p p p

p p p p p

p p p p p

p p p p p

Padre Pio

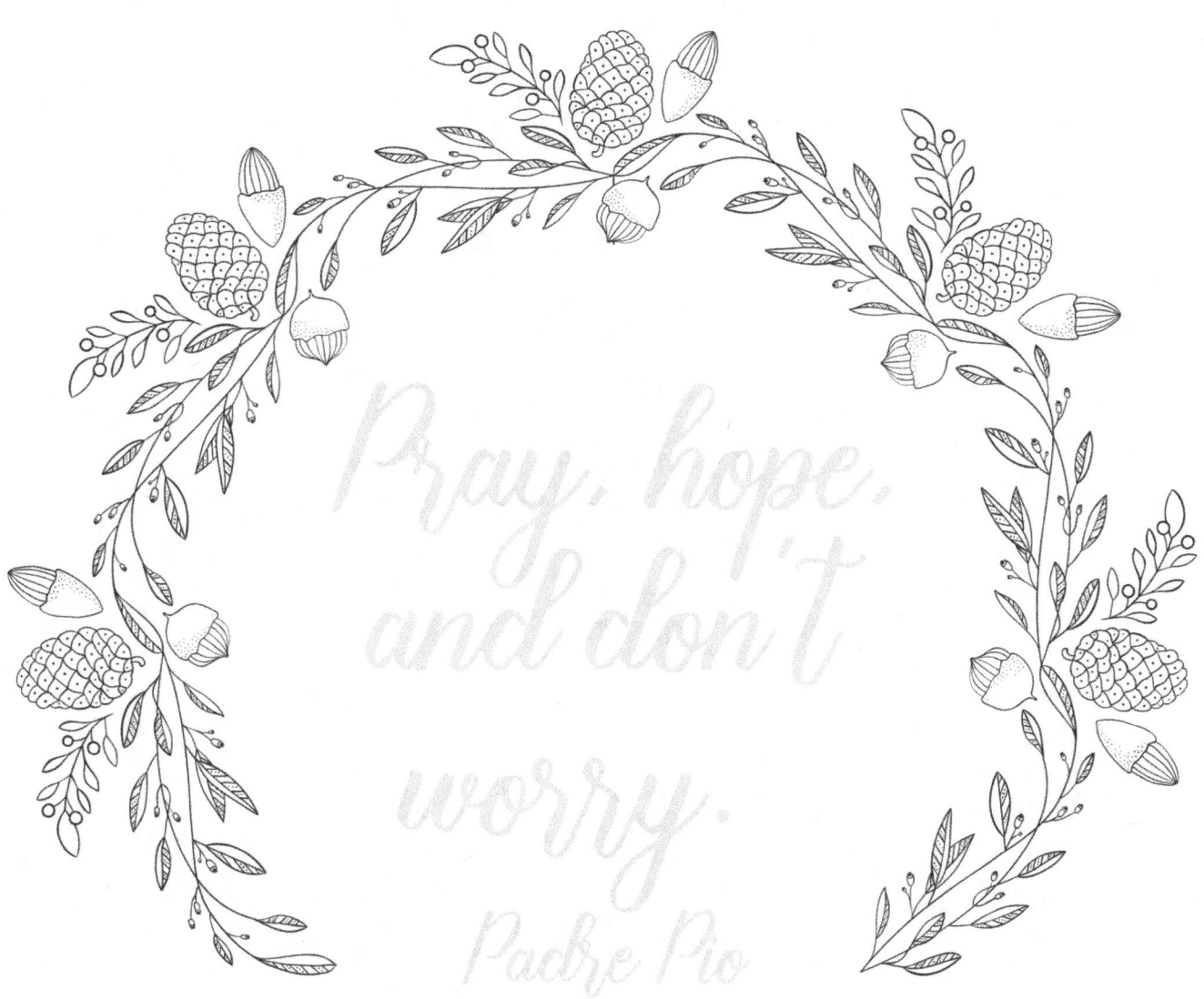

Pray, hope, and don't worry.
Padre Pio

Qq

Q Q Q Q Q

Q Q Q Q Q

q q q q q

q q q q q

Queen

Qq

Q Q Q Q Q

Q Q Q Q Q

q q q q q

q q q q q

Queen

I want to adorn myself, not out of worldly pride, but for love of God alone.
— Queen St Elizabeth of Hungary

Rr

R R R R R

R R R R R

r r r r r

r r r r r

Rose

Rr

R R R R R

R R R R R

r r r r r

r r r r r

Rose

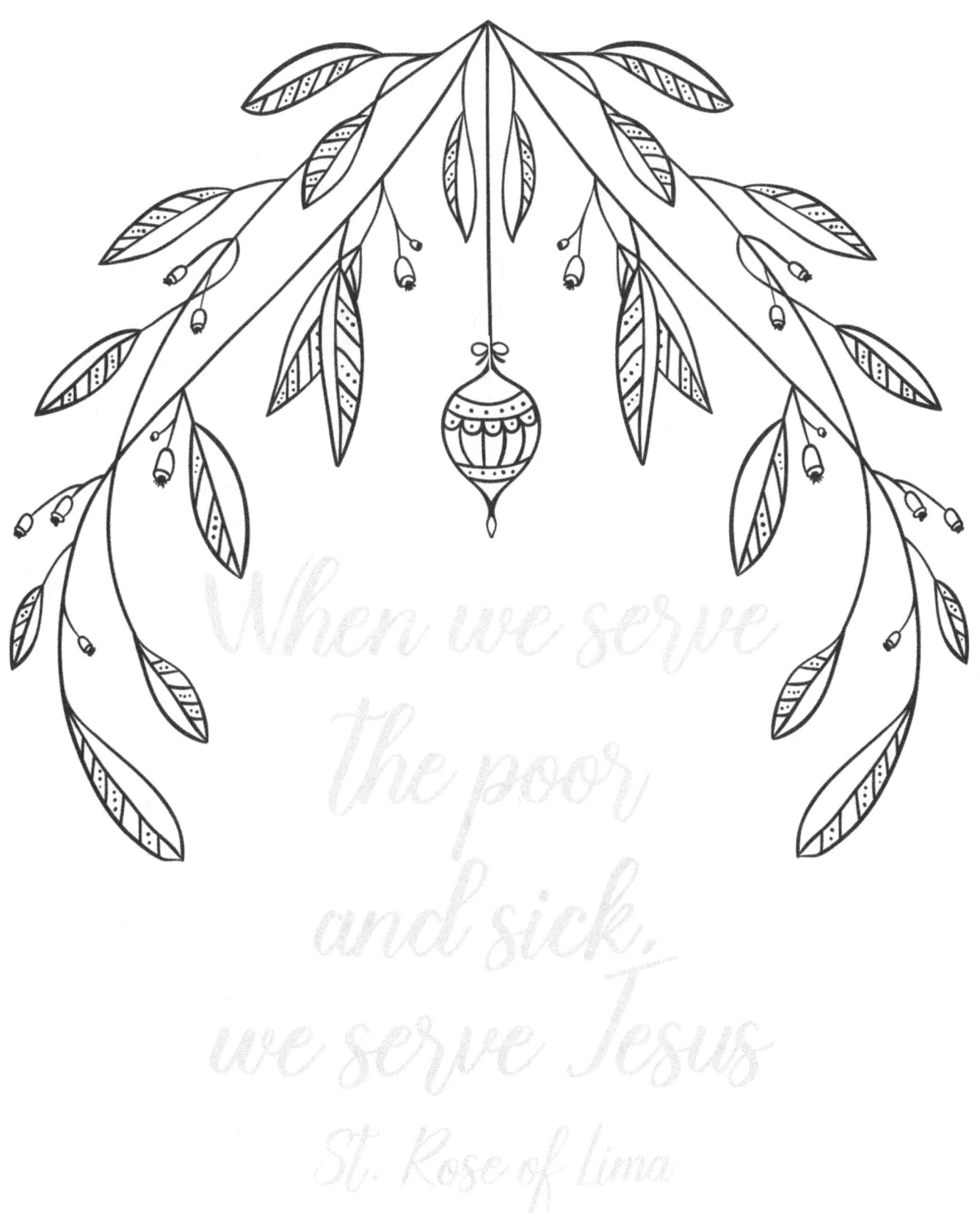

When we serve
the poor
and sick,
we serve Jesus
St. Rose of Lima

Ss

S S S S S

S S S S S

s s s s s

s s s s s

Stephen

Ss

S S S S S

S S S S S

s s s s s

s s s s s

Stephen

*Be humble
in this life,
that God may
raise you up
in the next.*
— St. Stephen

Tt

T T T T T

T T T T T

t t t t t

t t t t t

Therese

Tt

T T T T T

T T T T T

t t t t t

t t t t t

Therese

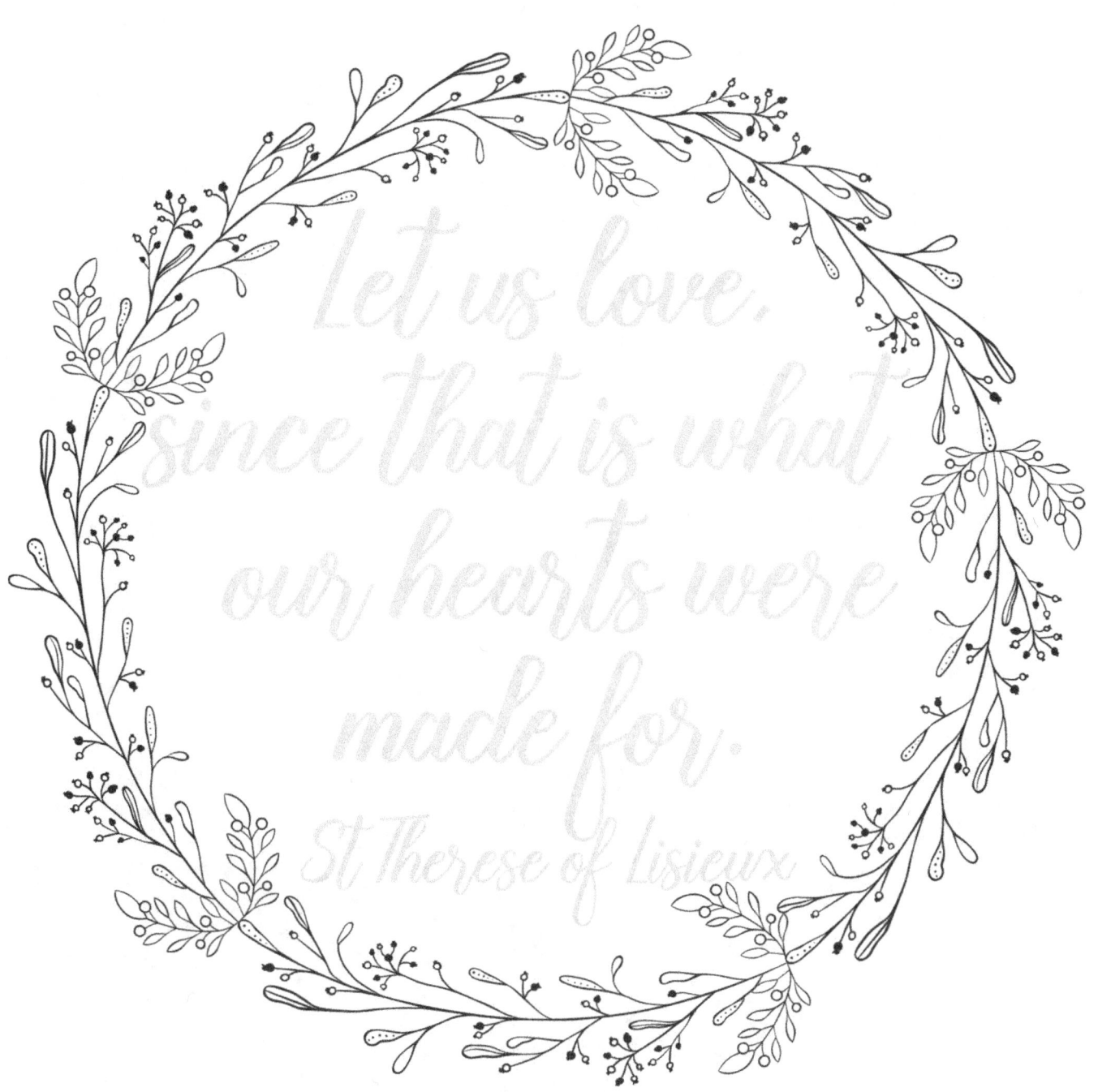

Uu

U U U U U

U U U U U

u u u u u

u u u u u

Ursula

Uu

U U U U U

U U U U U

u u u u u

u u u u u

Ursula

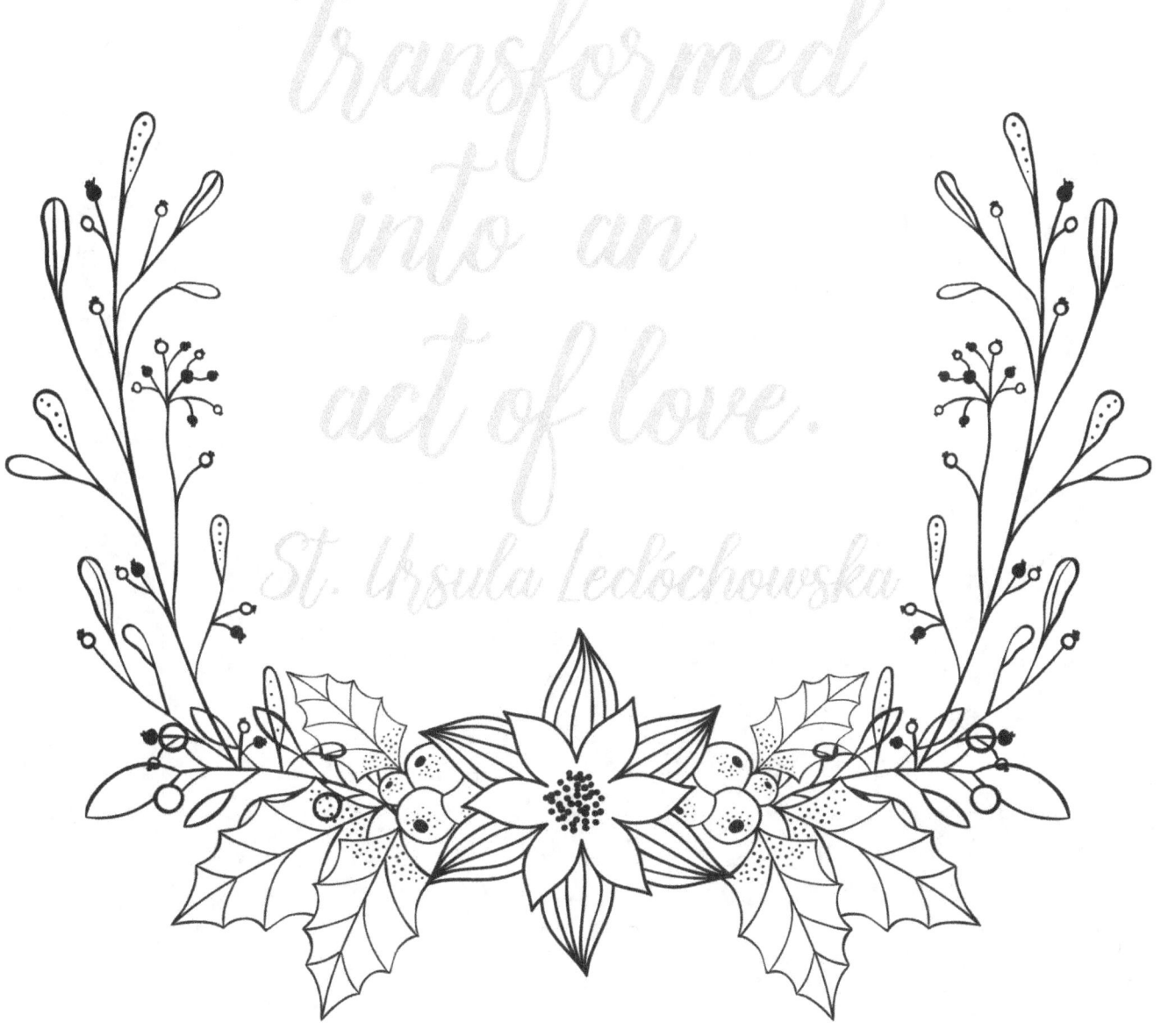

Every daily act
can be
transformed
into an
act of love.
St. Ursula Ledóchowska

The Fourth Week of Advent

Going Forward

Firstly, take a moment to appreciate the progress you've made. Look back to your first page. See how far you've come!

Even after you finish this Advent journey, keep practicing. Find small opportunities to bless others with your new skills. Handlettering adds a personal touch to Christmas cards, gift tags, and thank-you notes.

At the end of Advent, you'll also have spent this beautiful liturgical season resting in the wisdom of the Saints. By meditating daily on their words, you will fill your mind with truth, goodness, and lasting beauty.

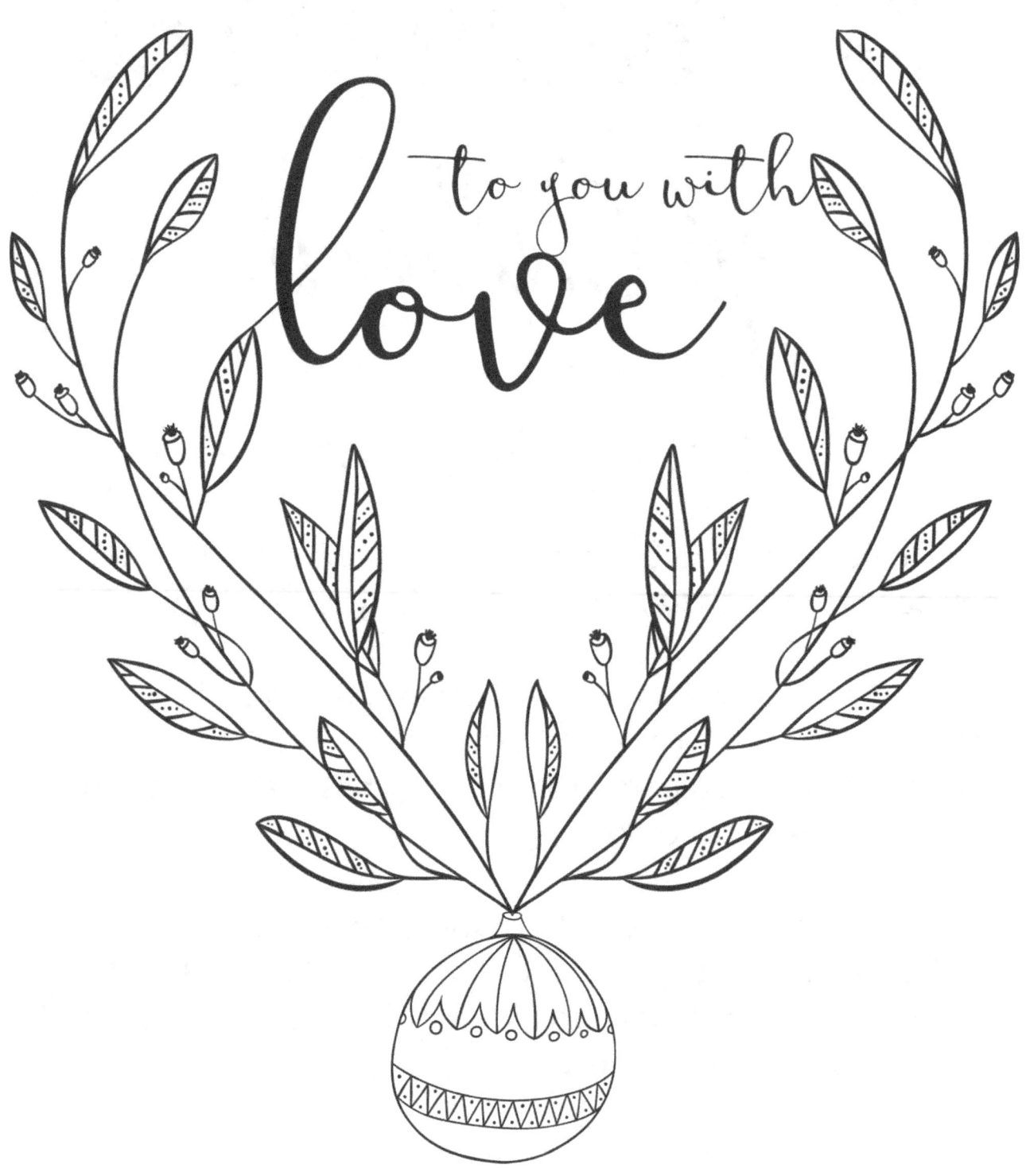

Vv

V V V V V

V V V V V

v v v v v

v v v v v

Vincent

Vv

V V V V V

V V V V V

v v v v v

v v v v v

Vincent

If we are faithful to God, we lack nothing.

St. Vincent de Paul

Ww

W W W W W

W W W W W

W W W W W

W W W W W

William

Ww

W W W W W
W W W W W
W W W W W
W W W W W

William

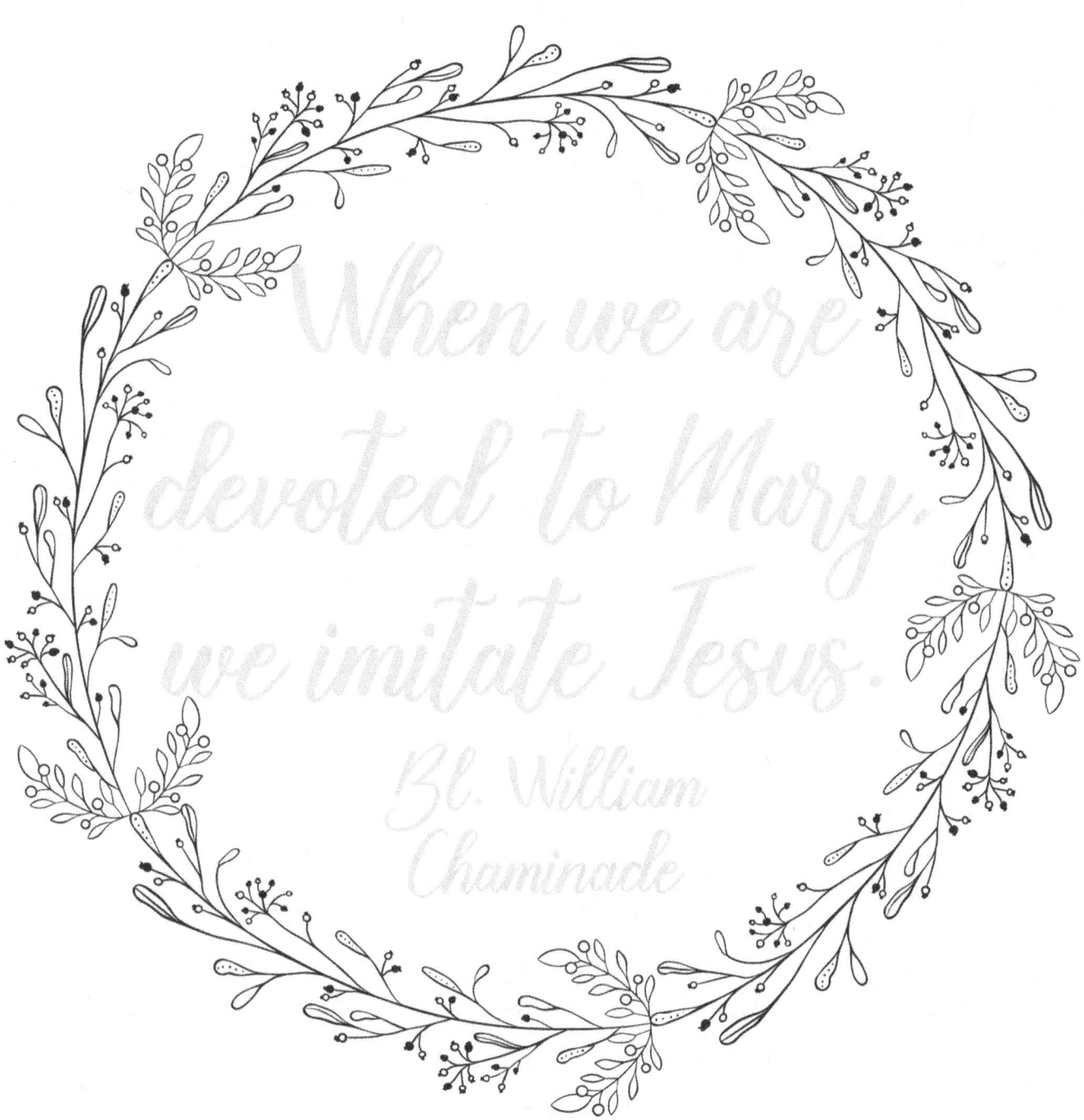

"When we are devoted to Mary, we imitate Jesus."
— Bl. William Chaminade

Xx

X X X X X

X X X X X

𝓍 𝓍 𝓍 𝓍 𝓍

𝓍 𝓍 𝓍 𝓍 𝓍

Xavier

Xx

X X X X X

X X X X X

x x x x x

x x x x x

Xavier

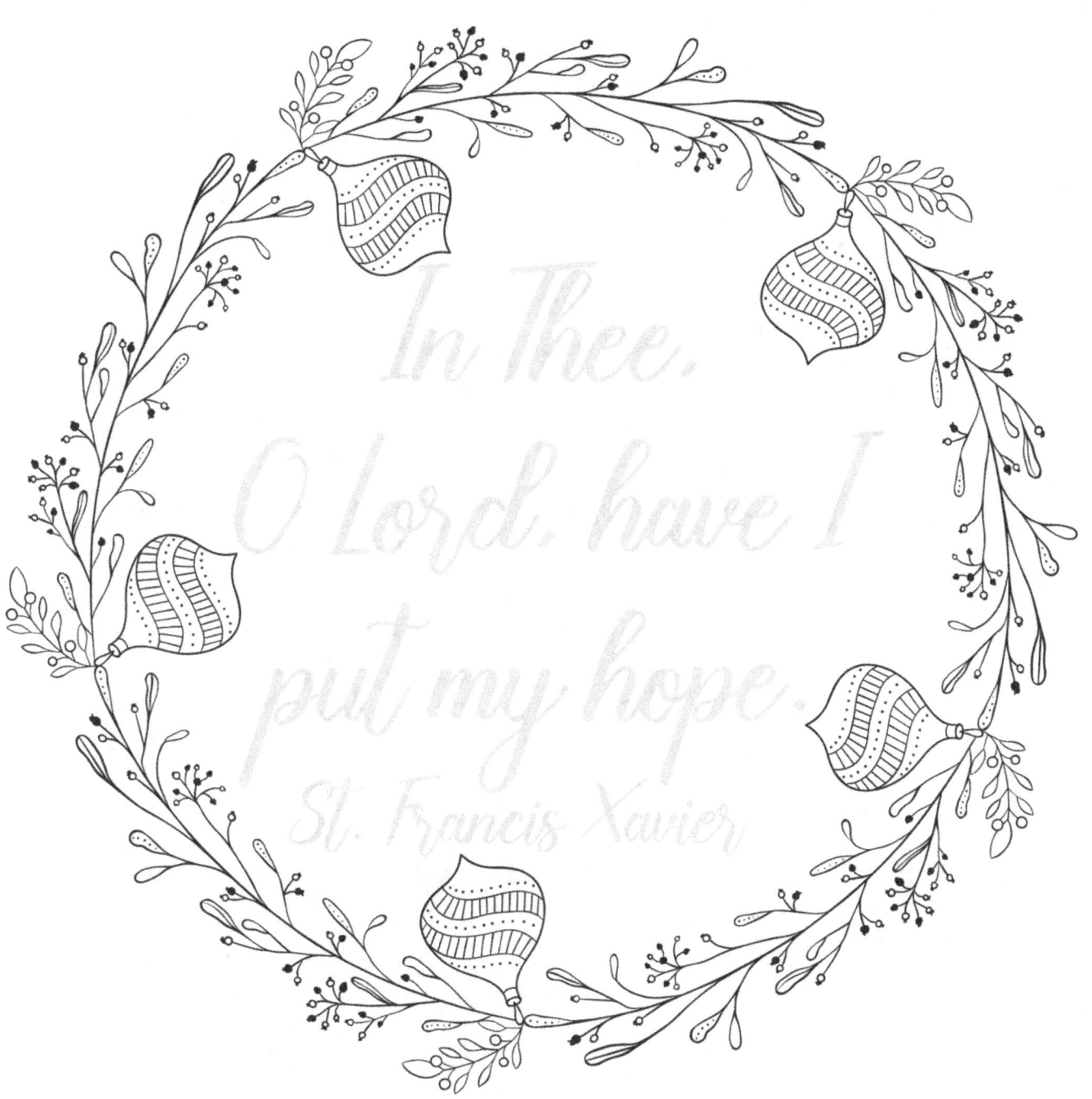

In Thee,
O Lord, have I
put my hope.
St. Francis Xavier

Yy

Y Y Y Y Y Y

Y Y Y Y Y Y

y y y y y y

y y y y y y

Yves

Yy

Y Y Y Y Y

Y Y Y Y Y

y y y y y

y y y y y

Yves

If you are willing to abandon the world, you will taste here on earth the joys of heaven.
St. St. Yves Hélory

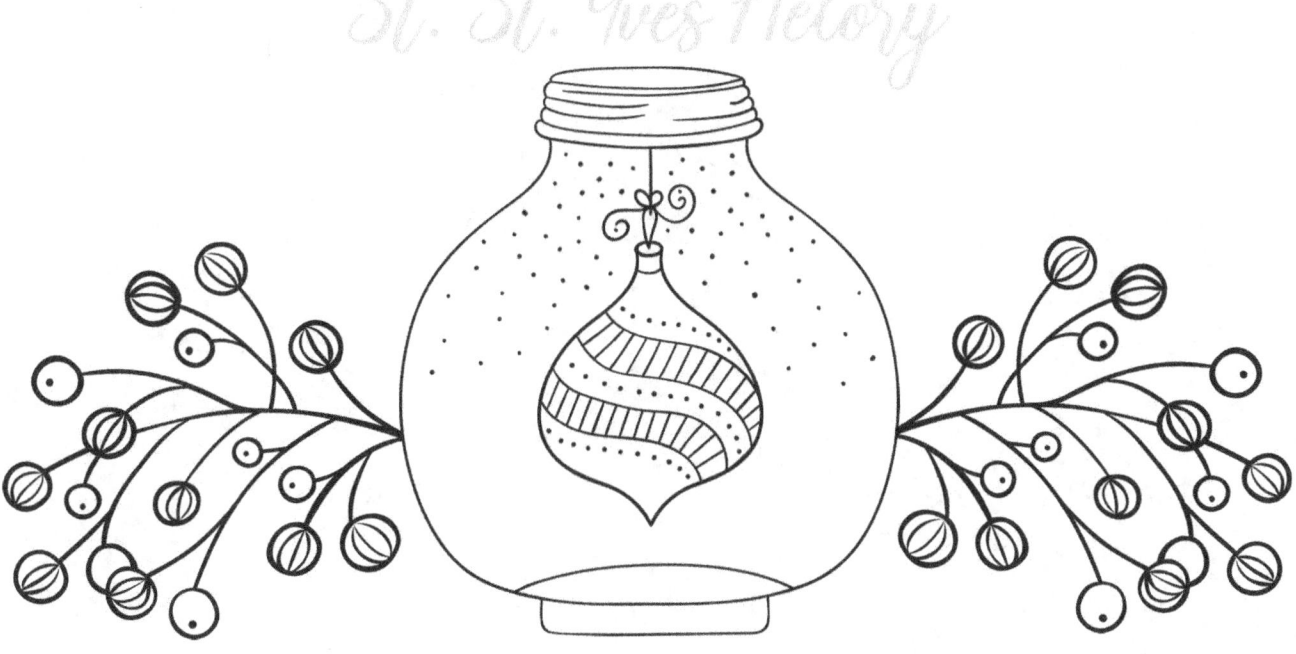

Zz

Z Z Z Z Z

Z Z Z Z Z

z z z z z

z z z z z

Zelie

Zz

Z Z Z Z Z

Z Z Z Z Z

z z z z z

z z z z z

Zelie

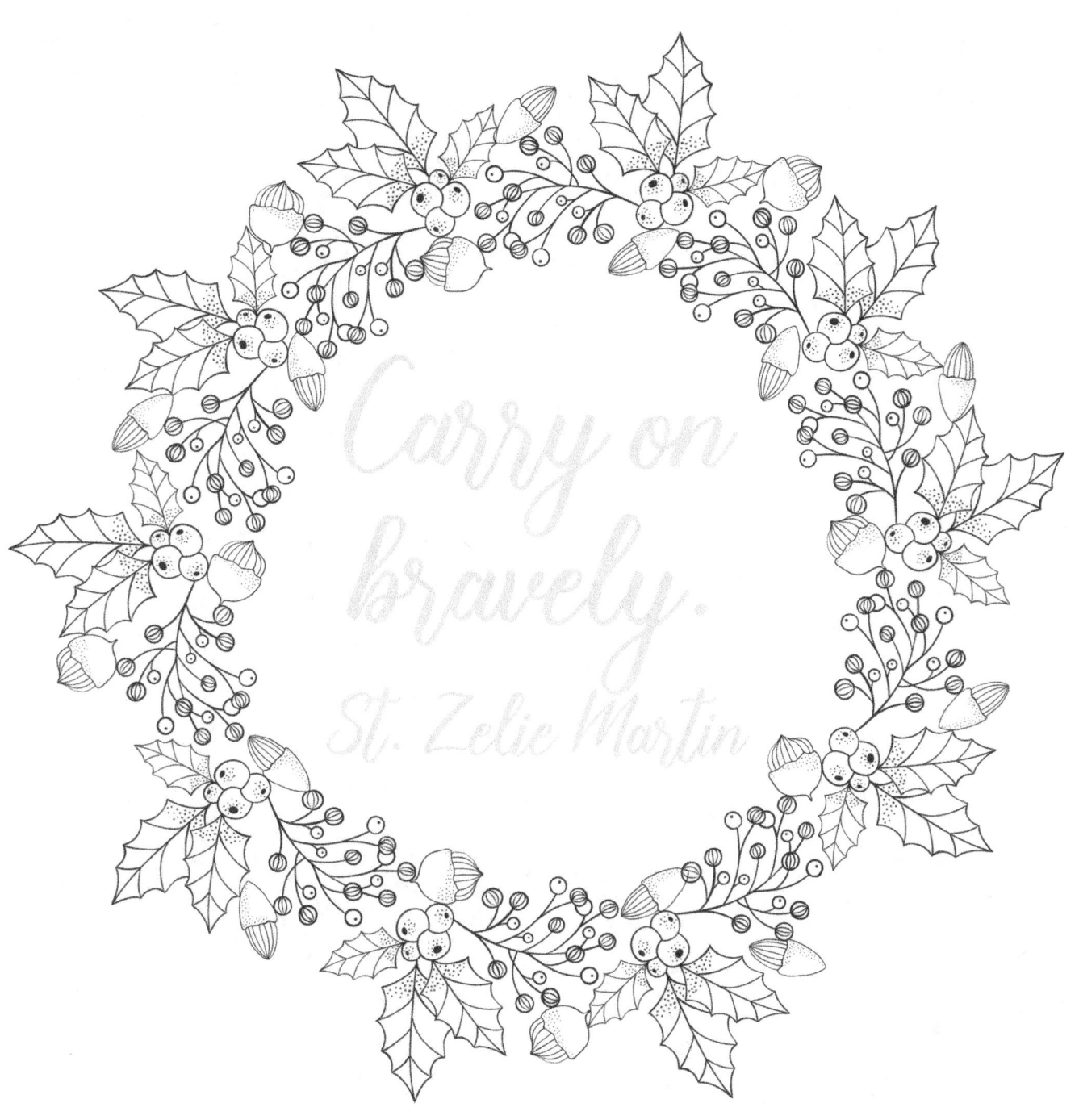

Extra Practice Pages

Use these pages to warm up or get extra practice with challenging letters. You can download and print more copies at www.booksfaithlife.com/practice

Extra Practice Pages

Aa Bb Cc Dd Ee

Ff Gg Hh Ii Jj Kk

Ll Mm Nn Oo Pp Qq

Rr Ss Tt Uu Vv Ww

Xx Yy Zz

Extra Practice Pages

Aa Bb Cc Dd Ee

Ff Gg Hh Ii Jj Kk

Ll Mm Nn Oo Pp Qq

Rr Ss Tt Uu Vv Ww

Xx Yy Zz

Extra Practice Pages

Aa Bb Cc Dd Ee

Ff Gg Hh Ii Jj Kk

Ll Mm Nn Oo Pp Qq

Rr Ss Tt Uu Vv Ww

Xx Yy Zz

Extra Practice Pages

Extra Practice Pages

Extra Practice Pages

www.ingramcontent.com/pod-product-compliance
Lightning Source LLC
Chambersburg PA
CBHW062325220526
45469CB00008B/2623